LINES ON THE UNDERGROUND

an anthology
for Circle Line travellers

Compiled by

DOROTHY MEADE & TATIANA WOLFF

Illustrated by Basil Cottle
and Jonathan Newdick

CASSELL

Cassell Publishers Limited
Wellington House, 125 Strand
London WC2R 0BB

in association with the London Transport Museum

Selection
copyright © Dorothy Meade and Tatiana Wolff 1994, 1996
Extracts copyright authors and publishers (see Acknowledgements)
Illustrations copyright © Basil Cottle and Jonathan Newdick 1994

This edition published 1996
The material in this anthology was first published in
Lines on the Underground, 1994

British Library Cataloguing in Publication Data
A catalogue record for this book is available from the British Library

ISBN 0-304-34904-6

Distributed in Australia by
Capricorn Link (Australia) Pty Ltd
2/13 Carrington Road, Castle Hill, NSW 2154

Printed and bound in Great Britain by Hillman Printers Ltd

To Joe, Dora, Anna and Ben

*

And in memory of
M. M. W.

CIRCLE LINE

Round *about*
And round *about*
And round *about I go.*

A.A. MILNE, 'Busy', *Now We Are Six*, 1927

King's Cross St. Pancras

Change for Hammersmith & City, Metropolitan, Northern,
Piccadilly and Victoria lines

King's Cross!
What shall we do?
His Purple Robe
Is rent in two!
Out of his Crown
He's torn the gems!
He's thrown his Sceptre
Into the Thames!
The Court is shaking
In its shoe –
King's Cross!
What shall we do?
Leave him alone
For a minute or two.

ELEANOR FARJEON,
Nursery Rhymes of London Town, 1916

1777. I remember well that in an autumn evening of this year . . .
going with [my father] and his pupils on a sketching party to what is
now called Pancras Old Church . . . which was at that time so rural
that it was only enclosed by a low and very old hand-railing, in some
parts entirely covered with docks and nettles.

J.T. SMITH, *A Book for a Rainy Day*, 1845

Bringing the line [of the Midland Railway] to London . . . was difficult
enough. . . . In order to do this the very large and very crowded burial
ground of old St. Pancras would have to be levelled. When the work
started, skulls and bones were seen lying about; a passer-by saw an
open coffin staved in through which peeped a bright tress of hair.
Great scandal was caused and the company was forced to arrange for
reverent reburial. The architect in charge of the reburial was A.W.
Blomfield, and he sent one of his assistants to watch the carrying away
of the dead to see that it was reverently done. That assistant was
Thomas Hardy, and his poems 'The Levelled Churchyard' and 'In the
Cemetery' recall the fact . . .

> O Passenger, pray list and catch
>   Our sighs and piteous groans,
> Half stifled in this jumbled patch
>   Of wrenched memorial stones!
>
> We late-lamented, resting here,
>   Are mixed to human jam,
> And each to each exclaims in fear,
>   'I know not which I am!'

Hardy never forgot the event.

JOHN BETJEMAN, *London's Historic Railway Stations*, 1972

*I have known a man, dying a long way from London, sigh queerly for a sight of
the gush of smoke that, on the platform of the Underground, one may see,
escaping in great woolly clots up a circular opening, by a grimy, rusted iron
shield, into the dim upper light. He wanted to see it again as others have wished
to see once more the Bay of Naples, the olive groves of Catania. But – alas perhaps – no man will ever see that sight again, for the Underground itself has
been 'electrified,' . . . and there is one of our glamours gone.*

FORD MADOX HUEFFER, *England and the English:*
An Interpretation, 1907

Farringdon

In mid-Victorian times [Farringdon Market] was celebrated for its cress. Mayhew paints a pathetic picture of the little watercress girls, some no more than seven years old, haggling with the saleswomen before dawn, then shivering in their cotton dresses and threadbare shawls as they tied up the bunches and washed the leaves at the pump before going out into the streets crying: 'Water-creases, four bunches a penny, water-creases!' On an average day they would make 3d or 4d.

The London Encyclopaedia edited by Ben Weinreb
and Christopher Hibbert, 1983

PUBLIC OPENING OF THE METROPOLITAN RAILWAY

On Saturday, from as early an hour as six o'clock in the morning until late at night, trains filled with people were running at short intervals of time between Paddington and Farringdon-street. It soon became apparent that the locomotive power and rolling stock at the disposal of the company was by no means in proportion to the requirements of the opening day. From eight o'clock or nine o'clock every station became crowded with intending travellers, who were admitted in sections; but poor were the chances of a place to those who ventured to take their tickets at any mid-way station, the occupants being, with but very rare exceptions, 'long distance' or terminus passengers. However, the crowding at King's-cross was immense. This station is certainly the finest on the line, throwing even the termini into the shade. Here the constant cry, as the trains arrived of 'No room!' appeared to have a very depressing effect upon those assembled. Between eleven and twelve at this station, and continuously for the space of an hour and a half, the money-takers refused to take money for passengers between King's-cross and Farringdon-street, but they issued tickets between that station and Paddington, and many, whose destination were Cityward, determined to ride on the railway on its first day of opening, took tickets for the opposite direction, in order to secure places for the return journey.

Daily Telegraph, 12 January 1863

Barbican

. . . under Henry III, the hostile Londoners built or strengthened several watch-towers, only to be forced to dismantle them after the king's triumph. . . . In 1377, with all the perils of a regency and a French invasion, it was decided to equip the gates with chains, portcullises and outer barbicans.

TIMOTHY BAKER, *Mediaeval London*, 1970

John Milton lived in the Barbican between 1645 and 1649. *L'Allegro* and *Comus* were probably written at this time. He was buried in St Giles without Cripplegate in the Barbican in 1674.

Moorgate
Change for Northern line

Often I longed to be in love; but I was already in love with London, and although too shy to go into pubs – and hating anyway the taste of beer – I would listen to the rattle of dominoes among the coffee tables of the Mecca as far north as Moorgate, and obscurely feel my passion.

V.S. PRITCHETT, *A Cab at the Door*, 1968

Snow falls in the buffet of Aldersgate station,
   Soot hangs in the tunnel in clouds of steam.
City of London! before the next desecration
   Let your steepled forest of churches be my theme. . . .

Snow falls in the buffet of Aldersgate station,
   Toiling and doomed from Moorgate Street puffs the train,
For us of the steam and the gas-light, the lost generation,
   The new white cliffs of the City are built in vain.

JOHN BETJEMAN, 'Monody on the Death of Aldersgate Street Station',
Collected Poems, 1958

Liverpool Street
Change for Central, Hammersmith & City and Metropolitan lines

After leaving the office I would travel either to Sloane Square or to Liverpool Street to have a drink in the station buffet. In the whole extension of the Underground system those two stations are, as far as I've been able to discover, the only ones which have bars actually upon the platform. The concept of the tube station platform bar excited me. In fact the whole Underground region moved me, I felt as if it were in some sense my natural home. These two bars were not just a cosy after-the-office treat, they were the source of a dark excitement, places of profound communication with London, with the sources of life, with the caverns of resignation to grief and to mortality. Drinking there between six and seven in the shifting crowd of rush-hour travellers, one could feel on one's shoulders as a curiously soothing yoke the weariness of toiling London. . . . The uncertainty of the order of the trains. The dangerousness of the platform. (Trains are lethal weapons.) The resolution of a given moment (but which?) to lay down your glass and mount the next train. . . . the stations, each unique, the sinister brightness of Charing Cross, the mysterious gloom of Regent's Park, the dereliction of Mornington Crescent, the futuristic melancholy of Moorgate, the monumental ironwork of Liverpool Street, the twining *art nouveau* of Gloucester Road, the Barbican sunk in a baroque hole, fit subject for Piranesi. And in the summer, like an excursion into the country, the flowering banks of the Westbound District Line . . . I loved the Inner Circle best.

IRIS MURDOCH, *A Word Child*, 1975

Aldgate

Know ye that we, with unanimous will and assent, have granted and released by these presents unto Geoffrey Chaucer the whole of the dwelling house above the gate of Algate, with the rooms built over, and a certain cellar beneath, the same gate, on the South side of that gate, and the appurtenances thereof, unto the aforesaid Geoffrey, for the whole life of him, the said Geoffrey.

Corporation of London Records Office, Letter-Book G, Fo. cccxxi,
part of the lease granting the whole of the house above
Aldgate to the poet Chaucer in 1374

> For when thy labour doon al ys,
> And hast mad alle thy rekenynges,
> In stede of reste and newe thynges,
> Thy goost hom to thy hous anoon,
> And, also domb as any stoon,
> Thou sittest at another book
> Tyl fully daswed ys thy look,
> And lyvest thus as an heremite,
> Although thyn abstynence ys lyte . . .

GEOFFREY CHAUCER, *The House of Fame*, describing his life in the house
above Aldgate between 1374 and 1385

Tower Hill
Change for District line

Jane called us up, about 3 in the morning, to tell us of a great fire they saw in the City. . . . So I made myself ready presently, and walked to the Tower and there got up upon one of the high places . . . and there I did see the houses at that end of the bridge all on fire, and an infinite great fire on this. . . . So down, with my heart full of trouble, to the Lieutenant of the Tower, who tells me that it begun this morning in the King's bakers house in Pudding Lane. . . . So I down to the water-side and there got a boat and through the bridge, and there saw a lamentable fire. . . . Everybody endeavouring to remove their goods, and flinging into the River or bringing them into lighters that lay off. Poor people staying in their houses as long as till the very fire touched them, and then running into boats or clambering from one pair of stairs by the waterside to another. And among other things, the poor pigeons I perceive were loath to leave their houses, but hovered about the windows and balconies till they were some of them burned, their wings

---

and fell down. . . . I observed that hardly one lighter or boat in three that had goods of a house in, but there was a pair of virginalls in it . . . I away to Whitehall by appointment . . . and walked to my boat, and there upon the water again, and to the fire up and down, it still increasing and the wind great. So near the fire as we could for smoke; and all over the Thames, with one's face in the wind you were almost burned with a shower of Firedrops . . . and saw the fire grow; and as it grow darker, appeared more and more, and in Corners and upon steeples and between churches and houses, as far as we could see up the hill of the City, in a most horrid malicious bloody flame, not like the fine flame of an ordinary fire. . . . We stayed till, it being darkish, we saw the fire as only one entire arch of fire from this to the other side of the bridge, and in a bow up the hill, for an arch of above a mile long. It made me weep to see it.

SAMUEL PEPYS, *Diary, Lords Day, 2 September 1666*

Monument
Change for escalator to Bank station for Central and Northern lines

The Monument, designed by Christopher Wren, commemorates the great fire of London of 1666.

. . . After dinner I sauntered in a pleasing humour to London Bridge, viewed the Thames's silver expanse and the springy bosom of the surrounding fields. I then went up to the top of the Monument. This is a most amazing building. It is a pillar two hundred feet high. In the inside, a turnpike stair runs up all the way. When I was about half way up, I grew frightened. I would have come down again, but thought I would despise myself for my timidity. Thus does the spirit of pride get the better of fear. I mounted to the top and got upon the balcony. It was horrid to find myself so monstrous a way up in the air, so far above London and all its spires. I durst not look round me. There is no real danger, as there is a strong rail both on the stair and balcony. But I shuddered, and as every heavy wagon passed down Gracechurch Street, dreaded that the shaking of the earth would make the tremendous pile tumble to the foundation. . . .

JAMES BOSWELL, *London Journal, 2 April 1763*

In the churches about Mark-lane . . . there was a dry whiff of wheat; and I accidentally struck an airy sample of barley out of an aged hassock in one of them. From Rood-lane to Tower-street, and thereabouts, there was often a subtle flavour of wine: sometimes, of tea. One church near Mincing-lane smelt like a druggist's drawer. Behind the Monument, the service had a flavour of damaged oranges, which, a little further down towards the river, tempered into herrings, and gradually toned into a cosmopolitan blast of fish.

CHARLES DICKENS in 'City of London Churches', *All the Year Round*,
5 May 1860, included in *The Uncommercial Traveller*, 1861

. . . one and sixpence. When I was your age, I had never seen so much money, in a heap. A shilling of it is in case of accidents – the mare casting a shoe, or the like of that. The other sixpence is to spend in the diversions of London; and the diversion I recommend is to go to the top of the Monument, and sitting there. There's no temptation there, sir – no drink – no young women – no bad characters of any sort – nothing but imagination. That's the way I enjoyed myself when I was your age, sir.

CHARLES DICKENS, *Barnaby Rudge*, 1841

Cannon Street

Then his gaze swept over [London] bridge to what could be seen beyond . . . cavernous, immense, the great black arch of Cannon Street Station, and high above, far beyond, not in the city but in the sky and still softly shining in the darkening air, a ball and a cross. It was the very top of St Paul's, seen above the roof of Cannon Street Station.

J.B. PRIESTLEY, *Angel Pavement*, 1930

Certainly London fascinates . . . the earth is explicable – from her we came, and we must return to her. But who can explain Westminster Bridge Road or Liverpool Street in the morning – the City inhaling – or the same thoroughfares in the evening – the City exhaling her exhausted air? . . .

The Londoner seldom understands his city until it sweeps him, too, away from his moorings.

E.M. FORSTER, *Howards End*, 1910

CADE: Now is Mortimer lord of this city. And here, sitting upon London-stone*, I charge and command that, of the city's cost, the pissing-conduit run nothing but claret wine this first year of our reign.

WILLIAM SHAKESPEARE, *Henry VI Part II*, 1591

*London Stone, the old Roman milestone, is now rounded with age, and set in a stone case built into the outer southern wall of the church of St Swithin, Cannon Street – the very stone that the arch-rebel Jack Cade struck with his bloody sword after storming London Bridge.

Mansion House

There was a dinner preparing at the Mansion House, and when I* peeped in at the grated kitchen window . . . my heart began to beat with hope that the Lord Mayor . . . would look out of an upper apartment and direct me to be taken in.

*Charles Dickens is here recollecting his own experience as a hungry nine-year-old.

CHARLES DICKENS, 'Gone Astray', *Household Words*, 1853

I love to return to London from the country, relieved on the terminus platform by the metropolitan excitement of so many people hurrying in so many ways – though in fact I will probably go straight home and not leave the house for a week. It is simply a feeling that one is in some sort of important swim; just as the availability of so many theatre and night amusements is comforting, though we very seldom use them. But if we lived in the country, there would, I am sure be a sense of deprivation.

WILLIAM SANSOM in *Living in London* edited by Alan Ross, 1974

April 30. Perfectly astounded at receiving an invitation for Carrie and myself from the Lord and Lady Mayoress to the Mansion House, to 'meet the Representatives of Trades and Commerce'. My heart beat like that of a schoolboy's. Carrie and I read the invitation over two or three times. I could scarcely eat my breakfast. I said – and felt it from the bottom of my heart – 'Carrie darling. I was a proud man when I led you down the aisle of the church on our wedding day; that pride will be equalled if not surpassed, when I lead my dear, pretty wife up to the Lord and Lady Mayoress at the Mansion House.'

GEORGE AND WEEDON GROSSMITH, *The Diary of a Nobody*, 1892

Blackfriars

And did you not hear of a jolly young waterman,
    Who at Blackfriars Bridge used for to ply;
And he feather'd his oars with such skill and dexterity,
    Winning each heart, and delighting each eye.
He look'd so neat, and he row'd so steadily:
The maidens all flock'd in his boat so readily,
And he ey'd the young rogues with so charming an air,
That this waterman ne'er was in want of a fare.

CHARLES DIBDIN, 'The Waterman', *The Songs of Charles Dibdin*, 1837

One of the loveliest glimpses of London I have ever seen is that which unfolds itself at night through the jet black arches of Blackfriars Bridge . . . the pin points of the Embankment lights curving round to Westminster across an oily expanse of Thames, the lights wavering in the water, and in the background, grey and sleeping, the tall buildings of the Embankment . . . a little oblong yellow tramcar moving slowly in the darkness. . . .

H.V. MORTON, *The Nights of London*, 1926

Temple

We then walked into the City, and then strolled about the Temple, which is a most agreeable place. You quit all the hurry and bustle of the City in Fleet Street and the Strand, and all at once find yourself in a pleasant academical retreat. You see good convenient buildings, handsome walks, you view the silver Thames. You are shaded by venerable trees. Crows are cawing above your head. Here and there you see a solitary bencher sauntering about.

JAMES BOSWELL, *London Journal*, 6 April 1763

I was born, and passed the first seven years of my life, in the Temple. Its church, its halls, its gardens, its fountain, its river, I had almost said – for in those young years, what was this king of rivers to me but a stream that watered our pleasant places? – these are of my oldest recollections. I repeat, to this day, no verses to myself more frequently, or with kindlier emotion, than those of Spenser, where he speaks of this spot:

> 'There when they came, whereas those bricky towers,
> The which on Themmes brode aged back doth ride,
> Where now the studious lawyers have their bowers,
> There whylome wont the Templar knights to bide,
> Till they decayed through pride.'

Indeed, it is the most elegant spot in the metropolis. What a transition for a countryman visiting London for the first time – the passing from the crowded Strand or Fleet Street, by unexpected avenues, into its magnificent ample squares, its classic green recesses!

CHARLES LAMB, 'The Old Benchers of the Inner Temple',
Essays of Elia, 1823

Embankment
Change for Bakerloo and Northern lines

I went crosse the Thames on the ice, now become so thick as to beare not only streetes of boothes, in which they roasted meate, and had divers shops of wares, quite acrosse as in a towne, but coaches, carts,and horses, passed over. I went from *Westminster stayres* to *Lambeth*, and dined with the Archbishop.

JOHN EVELYN, *Diary,* 9 January 1684

I determined to make my way down to the Embankment, and rest my eyes and cool my head by watching the variegated lights upon the river. Beyond comparison the night is the best time for this place; a merciful darkness hides the dirt of the waters, and the lights of this transition age, red, glaring orange, gas-yellow, and electric white, are set in shadowy outlines of every possible shade between grey and deep purple. Through the arches of Waterloo Bridge a hundred points of light mark the sweep of the Embankment, and above its parapet rise the towers of Westminster, warm grey against the starlight. The black river goes by with only a rare ripple breaking its silence, and disturbing the reflections of the lights that swim upon its surface.

H.G. WELLS, 'The Diamond Maker', *The Stolen Bacillus and Other Incidents,* 1895

Nature, or anything that reminds me of nature, disturbs me; it is too large, too complicated, above all too utterly pointless and incomprehensible. I am at home with the works of man; if I choose to set my mind to it, I can understand anything that any man has made or thought. That is why I always travel by Tube, never by bus if I can possibly help it. For, travelling by bus one can't avoid seeing, even in London, a few stray works of God – the sky, for example, an occasional tree, the flowers in the window-boxes. But travel by Tube and you see nothing but the works of man – iron riveted into geometrical forms, straight lines of concrete, patterned expanses of tiles. All is human and the product of friendly and comprehensible minds. All philosophies and all religions – what are they but spiritual Tubes bored through the universe! Through these narrow tunnels, where all is recognizably human, one travels comfortable and secure, contriving to forget that all round and below and above them stretches the blind mass of earth, endless and unexplored. Yes, give me the Tube and Cubismus every time; give me ideas, so snug and neat and simple and well made. And preserve me from nature.

ALDOUS HUXLEY, *Crome Yellow,* 1921

Westminster

We left London on Saturday morning at 1/2 past 5 or 6, the 31st of July . . . we mounted the Dover Coach at Charing Cross. It was a beautiful morning. The city, St. Paul's, with the river and a multitude of little boats, made a most beautiful sight as we crossed Westminster Bridge. The houses were not overhung by their cloud of smoke, and they were spread out endlessly, yet the sun shone so brightly, with such a fierce light, that there was even something like the purity of one of Nature's own grand spectacles.

DOROTHY WORDSWORTH, *The Journals*, 1802

Earth has not anything to show more fair:
Dull would he be of soul who could pass by
A sight so touching in its majesty:
This City now doth, like a garment, wear
The beauty of the morning; silent, bare,
Ships, towers, domes, theatres, and temples lie
Open unto the fields, and to the sky;
All bright and glittering in the smokeless air.
Never did sun more beautifully steep
In his first splendour, valley, rock, or hill;
Ne'er saw I, never felt, a calm so deep!
The river glideth at his own sweet will:
Dear God! the very houses seem asleep;
And all that mighty heart is lying still!

WILLIAM WORDSWORTH, 'Composed upon
Westminster Bridge, September 3, 1802'

The actors know their parts. The public crowd who wait for the Speaker's Procession which passes every day through the light Central Hall [of Westminster] have a homely and ludicrous look in this gay Gothic setting; for the defect of a Gothic background is that it makes twentieth-century man and woman look vulgar and pathetic. The scene may have been more tolerable in the Victorian age, when clothes were severer, or more elaborate than they are now; but even then one must have felt the human inadequacy in these surroundings. . . . But when, suddenly, a loud voice calls out, 'The Speaker', and another voice calls out sharply, 'Hats off', there is a silence in which one realizes that what is about to happen is not a joke at all. One is going to see the ghosts walk. One hears their rapid step. They go by in their black with the briskness of a dream and give a cold thrill for a second or two to the blood. Exactly at half past two, in perfect step, expressionless, chins a little raised, as if on some duty, exalted and exquisitely unnecessary, five men go by, dressed in black: the Sergeant-at-Arms; the mace-bearer, holding the mace before him; the wigged Speaker himself, in black silk knee-breeches and buckled shoes; his train-bearer, holding up his short robe; and his chaplain, bringing up the rear. A stir of air follows them. They have vanished. The strange moment, with no clowning in it, is eerie; it is one of London's brilliant little set pieces. In twenty seconds the 'thing' has been 'done'.

V.S. PRITCHETT, *London Perceived*, 1962

Sir Joshua Reynolds (1723–92) commented of Westminster Abbey as long as 200 years ago: 'Westminster is already so stuffed with statuary it would be a deadly sin against taste to increase the squeeze of tombs there.'

> *I love to think of bland Pall Mall*
> *(Where Charles made love to pretty Nell)*
> *And rich South Audley Street, and Wapping,*
> *And Bond Street, and the Christmas shopping.*
> *Knightsbridge, the Inner Circle train,*
> *And Piccadilly and Park Lane.*

DOUGLAS GOLDRING, 'In Praise of London',
Streets and Other Verses, 1920

St. James's Park

Me thinks I see the love that shall be made,
The Lovers walking in that Amorous shade,
The Gallants dancing by the Rivers side,
They bath in Summer, and in Winter slide.
Methinks I hear the Musick in the boats,
And the loud Eccho which returnes the notes,
Whilst over head a flock of new sprung fowle
Hangs in the aire, and does the Sun controle:
Darkning the aire they hover o'er, and shrowd
The wanton Saylors with a feather'd cloud.
The Ladies angling in the Cristal lake,
Feast on the water with the prey they take.
A thousand Cupids on the billows ride,
And Sea-nimphs enter with the swelling tyde . . .

EDMUND WALLER, *A Poem on St James's Park*
As lately improved by his Maiesty, 1661

My walk to town to-day . . . was prodigiously hot: . . . it is two good miles, and just five thousand seven hundred and forty-eight steps; . . . When I pass the Mall in the evening it is prodigious to see the number of ladies walking there; and I always cry shame at the ladies of Ireland, who never walk at all, as if their legs were of no use, but to be laid aside. . . . Do you know that about our town we are mowing already and making hay, and it smells so sweet as we walk through the flowery meads; but the hay-making nymphs are perfect drabs, nothing so clean and pretty as further in the country. There is a mighty increase of dirty wenches in straw hats since I knew London.

JONATHAN SWIFT, from letter XXIII, 15–19 May 1711,
The Journal to Stella, 1768

Victoria

Change for Victoria and District lines

LADY BRACKNELL: Found!

JACK: The late Mr. Thomas Cardew, an old gentleman of a very charitable and kindly disposition, found me, and gave me the name of
Worthing, because he happened to have a first-class ticket for
Worthing in his pocket at the time. Worthing is a place in Sussex. It
is a seaside resort.

LADY BRACKNELL: Where did the charitable gentleman who had a first-
class ticket for this seaside-resort find you?

JACK (gravely): In a hand-bag.

LADY BRACKNELL: A hand-bag?

JACK (very seriously): Yes, Lady Bracknell. I was in a hand-bag – a
somewhat large, black leather hand-bag, with handles to it – an
ordinary hand-bag in fact.

LADY BRACKNELL: In what locality did this Mr James, or Thomas,
Cardew come across this ordinary hand-bag?

JACK: In the cloakroom at Victoria Station. It was given to him in mistake for his own.

LADY BRACKNELL: The cloak-room at Victoria Station?

JACK: Yes. The Brighton line.

LADY BRACKNELL: The line is immaterial. Mr Worthing, I confess I feel
somewhat bewildered by what you have just told me. To be born,
or at any rate bred, in a hand-bag, whether it had handles or not,
seems to me to display a contempt for the ordinary decencies of
family life that reminds one of the worst excesses of the French
Revolution. And I presume you know what that unfortunate move-
ment led to? As for the particular locality in which the hand-bag
was found, a cloak-room at a railway station might serve to conceal
a social indiscretion – has probably, indeed, been used for that pur-
pose before now – but it could hardly be regarded as an assured
basis for a recognised position in good society. . . . You can hardly
imagine that I and Lord Bracknell would dream of allowing our
only daughter – a girl brought up with the utmost care – to marry
into a cloak-room, and form an alliance with a parcel.

OSCAR WILDE, *The Importance of Being Earnest*, 1895

The flashiest of all suburban travellers are those who travel daily from
Victoria by first-class Pullman trains to Brighton. Indeed, Brighton so

dominates Victoria Station that though continental trains depart from
its South Eastern Section, though many of the inner London suburbs
are served by puzzling loop lines which start here and end at London
Bridge, Victoria is the station of what moneyed leisure is left in
London. Though it is meant to be associated with the South Coast and
summer holidays, the sea is not what one associates with those who
use it regularly. They do not look as though they took a winter dip in
the English Channel. Warm flats, television, cocktail cabinets and
bridge seem to be more in their line.

JOHN BETJEMAN, 'London Railway Stations',
Flower of Cities: A Book of London, 1949

Sloane Square

Soames used the Underground again in going home. The fog was
worse than ever at Sloane Square Station. Through the still, thick blur,
men groped in and out; women, very few, grasped their reticules to
their bosoms and handkerchiefs to their mouths; crowned with the
weird excrescence of the driver, haloed by a vague glow of lamp-light
that seemed to drown in vapour before it reached the pavement, cabs
loomed dim-shaped ever and again, and discharged citizens bolting like
rabbits to their burrows.

And these shadowy figures, wrapped each in his own little shroud
of fog, took no notice of each other. In the great warren, each rabbit
for himself, especially those clothed in the more expensive fur, who,
afraid of carriages on foggy days, are driven underground.

JOHN GALSWORTHY, <i>The Man of Property</i>, 1906

They knew what they meant to do. They were going to have their money's
worth, and far more than their money's worth, of underground travelling.
Round and round and round and all for a penny fare. . . . This was a favourite
occupation of theirs, a secret, morbid vice. They indulged in it at least twice
every holidays. . . .

Sloane Square. Two penny fares. Down the stairs into the delicious, roman-
tic, cool valley. The train thundered in. Inner Circle its style. A half empty com-
partment; there was small run on the underground this lovely August Sunday.
Into it dashed the children; they had a corner seat each, next the open door.
They bumped up and down on the seats, opposite each other. The train speeded

off, rushing like a mighty wind. South Kensington station. More people coming in, getting out. Off again. Gloucester Road, High Street, Notting Hill Gate, Queen's Road. . . . The penny fare was well over. Still they travelled, and jogged up and down on the straw seats, and chanted softly, monotonously, so that they could scarcely be heard above the roaring of the train:

> *. . . Where great whales come sailing by,*
> *Sail and sail with unshut eye,*
> *Round the world for ever and aye,*
> *ROUND THE WORLD FOR EVER AND AYE . . .*

At Paddington they saw the conductor eyeing them, and changed their compartment. This should be done from time to time.

And so on, past King's Cross and Farringdon Street, towards the wild, romantic stations of the east: Liverpool Street, Aldgate, and so round the bend, sweeping west like the sun. Blackfriars, Temple, Charing Cross, Westminster, St James's Park, Victoria, SLOANE SQUARE. O joy! Sing for the circle completed, the new circle begun.

> *. . . Where great whales come sailing by . . .*
> *ROUND THE WORLD FOR EVER AND AYE . . .*

ROSE MACAULAY, *Told by an Idiot*, 1923

South Kensington
Change for Piccadilly line

It is no longer true to think of South Kensington as was the habit to think of it not long ago, as a region ineffably English, where afternoon tea, the Times crossword, dogs and dinner jackets each prevailed at their appointed hour; where military and civilian vertebrae from the backbone of the British Empire came to retirement in private hotels. . . .

NICOLAS BENTLEY in *Flower of Cities. A Book of London. Studies and Sketches by Twenty-two Authors*, 1949

. . . an elderly lady of ample proportions found it necessary to alight from a narrow 3rd class compartment in reverse, with her back to the platform. The guard saw her in this position, half in and half out of the compartment, and concluded that she was trying to board the train – so he gave her a helping push. It is said that she travelled the whole Inner Circle, being pushed back into the train at each station, before the guard realised his mistake.

HENRY HOWSON, *London's Underground*, 1951

Gloucester Road
Change for District and Piccadilly lines

Oh dear, and a very big 'oh dear' at that. Rumpole's occupation, that of making sure that citizens of all classes are not randomly convicted of crimes they didn't do just so that the prison statistics may look more impressive, seems to have fallen into disrepute. I felt more than usually unappreciated as I burrowed down the Gloucester Road tube on my mole-like journey to irritate the constabulary and pour sand in the gear-box of justice, and when I emerged, blinking, into the daylight of the Temple Station I was beginning to wonder if it was not time to abandon the up-hill struggle. Was it possible that Rumpole should retire from the Bar?

JOHN MORTIMER, 'Rumpole and the Age of Retirement',
The Trials of Rumpole, 1979

High Street Kensington

Where *Kensington* high o'er the neighb'ring lands
'Midst greens and sweets, a Regal fabrick stands,
And sees each spring, luxuriant in her bowers,
A snow of blossoms, and a wilde of flowers,
The Dames of Britain oft in crowds repair
To gravel walks, and unpolluted air.
Here, while the Town in damps and darkness lies,
They breathe in sun-shine, and see azure skies;
Each walk, with robes of various dyes bespread,
Seems from afar a moving Tulip-bed,
Where rich Brocades and glossy Damasks glow,
And Chints, the rival of the show'ry Bow.

THOMAS TICKELL, *Kensington Garden*, 1722

The Albert Memorial, therefore, will not only be very beautiful, but also the most remarkable and interesting object in England, if not in Europe. . . . It stands in an elegant garden, and, with the Albert Hall, will make two magnificent objects, and still further ornament the already fine approach to Kensington.

ISABELLA BURT, *Historical Notices of Chelsea, Kensington,
Fulham, and Hammersmith*, 1871

Notting Hill Gate
Change for Central line

'I'm glad you are so stalwart a defender of your old inviolate Notting Hill. Look up nightly to that peak, my child, where it lifts itself among the stars so ancient, so lonely, so unutterably Notting. So long as you are ready to die for the sacred mountain, even if it were ringed with all the armies of Bayswater – ' The King stopped suddenly, and his eyes shone.

'Perhaps,' he said, 'perhaps the noblest of all my conceptions. A revival of the arrogance of the old mediaeval cities applied to our glorious suburbs. Clapham with a city guard. Wimbledon with a city wall. Surbiton tolling a bell to raise its citizens. West Hampstead going into battle with its own banner. . . .'

G.K. CHESTERTON, *The Napoleon of Notting Hill*, 1904

Wyndham Lewis remarked to me that he, at any rate, as an author had 'never found it safe to live more than ten minutes away from Notting Hill Gate'.

GEOFFREY GRIGSON in *Coming to London*
edited by John Lehmann, 1957

In a Tube train, for instance, Ben could sit with his eyes shut for the whole journey, and if anyone noticed, no one commented. He felt especially safe if he could allow himself to be caught by the rush-hour, and in the Inner Circle Tube. The other passengers, sitting or strap-hanging or simply wedged upright by the pressure of the crowd, endured their journey with their eyes shut – you see them so, travelling home at the end of any working-day in London. Like them, Ben kept his eyes shut, but he was not tired. . . . No one ever saw what he was seeing: a fawn-coloured dog of incredible minuteness.

If Ben was sitting, he saw the dog on his knee. If he stood, he looked down with his shut eyes and saw it at his feet. The dog was always with him, only dashing ahead or lingering behind in order to play tricks of agility and daring. When Ben finally left the Tube train, for instance, the Chihuahua would play that dangerous game of being last through the closing doors. When Ben rode up the Up escalator with his eyes shut, the Chihuahua chose to run up the Down one, and always arrived at the top first. . . .

PHILIPPA PEARCE, *A Dog So Small*, 1962

Bayswater

A trick that everyone abhors
In Little Girls is slamming doors.
A Wealthy Banker's Little Daughter
Who lived in Palace Green, Bayswater
(By name Rebecca Offendort),
Was given to this Furious Sport.
She would deliberately go
And Slam the door like Billy-ho!
To make her Uncle Jacob start.
She was not really bad at heart,
But only rather rude and wild:
She was an aggravating child.

HILAIRE BELLOC, 'Rebecca, who slammed doors for fun and
perished miserably', *Cautionary Tales for Children*, 1907

He [James Forsyte] took the slanting path from the Bayswater side of
the Row to Knightsbridge Gate, across a pasture of short, burnt grass,
dotted with blackened sheep, strewn with seated couples and strange
waifs lying prone on their faces, like corpses on a field over which the
wave of battle has rolled.

J. GALSWORTHY, *The Man of Property*, 1906

Now that we are wedged together,
Sweet stranger,
Closer than man and wife,
Why not make the best of this indignity?
Let our blood rioting together,
Murmur stories of our life's adventures,
Just as a river in its course
Brings emblems from its source.

Swing! Swing!
We are shamed, abashed:
Thrown breast to breast.
You dare not look in my eyes
Nor I in yours.

And yet in spite of this
I feel strange sympathies
Bearing my heart back
Along some time-tunnelling track
Which I do not recognize
Which I never trod before.
Swing! Swing!
The crowd is wheat
Before the scythe.
You are swept off your feet,
Thrown against me, a wave,
Dashed on a rock.
But we survive the shock.

RICHARD CHURCH, 'Strap-hanging',
Mood without Measure, 1928

Paddington
Change for Bakerloo and Hammersmith & City lines

The undergraduates of Oxford used Paddington; and so did Public Schools at Eton, Radley, Marlborough, Shrewsbury, Malvern and the now extinct Weymouth College; hunting people got out at Badminton; carpet manufacturers at Kidderminster; coal owners at Cardiff, jewellers at Birmingham; valetudinarians at Torquay, Leamington, Cheltenham, Tenbury Wells and Tenby, sailors at Plymouth, Devonport and Falmouth; organists used it for the Three Choirs Festival at Worcester, Hereford and Gloucester. The Welsh, who seem so often to be in trains, use it all the time.

JOHN BETJEMAN, *London's Historic Railway Stations*, 1972

Mr. and Mrs. Brown first met Paddington on a railway platform. In fact, that was how he came to have such an unusual name for a bear, for Paddington was the name of the station.

The Browns were there to meet their daughter. . . . It was a warm summer day and the station was crowded with people on their way to the seaside. Trains were whistling, taxis hooting, porters rushing about shouting at one another, and altogether there was so much noise that

Mr. Brown, who saw him first, had to tell his wife several times before she understood.

'A *bear*? On Paddington Station?' Mrs. Brown looked at her husband in amazement. 'Don't be silly, Henry. There can't be!' . . .

. . . The bear raised its hat politely – twice. 'I haven't really got a name,' he said. 'Only a Peruvian one which no one can understand.'

'Then we'd better give you an English one,' said Mrs. Brown. 'It will make things much easier.' She looked round the station for inspiration. 'It ought to be something special,' she said thoughtfully. As she spoke an engine standing in one of the platforms gave a loud whistle and let off a cloud of steam. 'I know what!' she exclaimed. 'We found you on Paddington Station so we'll call you Paddington!'

MICHAEL BOND, *A Bear Called Paddington*, 1958

. . . the fine flare of one of Mr W.H. Smith's bookstalls – a feature not to be omitted in my enumeration of the charms of Paddington and Euston. It is a focus of warmth and light in the vast smoky cavern; it gives the idea that literature is a thing of splendour, of a dazzling essence, of infinite gas-lit red and gold. A glamour hangs over the glittering booth and a tantalising air of clever new things. How brilliant must the books all be, how veracious and courteous the fresh, pure journals! Of a Saturday afternoon, as you wait in your corner of the compartment for the starting of the train, the window makes a frame for the glowing picture.

HENRY JAMES, *English Hours*, 1905

Edgware Road

Yesterday Mary Anne and I made our first trip down the 'Drain'. We walked to the Edgware Road and took first class tickets for King's Cross (6d each). We experienced no disagreeable odour, beyond the smell common to tunnels. The carriages hold ten persons, with divided seats, and are lighted by gas (two lights), they are also so lofty that a six footer may stand erect with his hat on. Trains run every 15 minutes from six in the morning till twelve at night (with some slight variation), and about 30,000 are conveyed on the line daily: shares have risen, and there is a prospect of a large dividend. Monday, 26 January 1863.

SIR WILLIAM HARDMAN, *A Mid-Victorian Pepys: The Letters and Memoirs of Sir William Hardman* edited by S.M. Ellis, 1923

Baker Street

Change for Bakerloo, Jubilee and Metropolitan lines

. . . At this moment there was a loud ring at the bell and I could hear Mrs. Hudson, our landlady, raising her voice in a wail of expostulation and dismay.

'By heavens, Holmes,' said I, half rising, 'I believe that they are really after us.'

'No, it's not quite so bad as that. It is the unofficial force – the Baker Street irregulars.'

As he spoke, there came a swift pattering of naked feet upon the stairs, a clatter of high voices, and in rushed a dozen dirty and ragged little street arabs. There was some show of discipline among them, despite their tumultuous entry, for they instantly drew up in line and stood facing us with expectant faces. One of their number, taller and older than the others, stood forward with an air of lounging superiority which was very funny in such a disreputable little scarecrow.

'Got your message, sir,' said he, 'and brought 'em on sharp. Three bob and a tanner for tickets.'

'Here you are,' said Holmes, producing some silver. 'In future they can report to you, Wiggins and you to me. I cannot have the house invaded in this way. . . .'

'. . . Look here, Watson; you look regularly done. Lie down there on the sofa, and see if I can put you to sleep.'

He took up his violin from the corner, and as I stretched myself out he began to play some low, dreamy, melodious air – his own, no doubt, for he had a remarkable gift for improvisation. I have a vague remembrance of his gaunt limbs, his earnest face and the rise and fall of his bow. Then I seemed to be floated peacefully away upon a soft sea of sound, until I found myself in dreamland. . . .

SIR ARTHUR CONAN DOYLE, *The Sign of Four*, 1890

During the Second World War, Baker Street housed the Headquarters of the SOE (Special Operations Executive), a secret service organisation from 1940 to 1946 organising underground warfare and sabotage against Germany and her allies.

Great Portland Street

. . . Another difficulty was ridding the tunnels of smoke from the steam engines which were used before the introduction of electric locomotion at the end of the century. Special engines were developed to condense the smoke, but the Metropolitan's cheery statement that the atmosphere in the tunnels was usually clear enough to enable drivers to see the signals cannot have been entirely reassuring. Nor did the general manager's suggestion that a visit to Great Portland Street station would bring instant relief to bronchitis sufferers carry much conviction.

ROBERT GRAY, *A History of London*, 1978

Euston Square

The ground behind the north-west end of Russell Street [i.e. Euston Square] was occupied by a farm occupied by two old maiden sisters of the name of Capper. They wore riding-habits, and men's hats; one rode an old grey mare, and it was her spiteful delight to ride with a large pair of shears after boys who were flying their kites, purposely to cut their strings; the other sister's business was to seize the clothes of the lads who trespassed on their premises to bathe.

J.T. SMITH, *A Book for a Rainy Day*, 1905 edition

It stood out . . . that when you came to look into things in a spirit of earnestness an immense deal could be done for very little more than your fare in the Underground.

HENRY JAMES, *What Maisie Knew*, 1897

ACKNOWLEDGEMENTS

We would like to thank our families and friends who have helped us over the years during the preparation of this book, especially Sandy Marriage, Robin Ollington, Bryan Rooney, Suzanne St Albans, Anthony Sampson, Kathleen Tillotson, Malcolm Holmes of the Camden Local History Library and the staff of the North Reading Room, British Library.

The compilers and publishers gratefully acknowledge permission to reproduce the following copyright material in this book:

Timothy Baker: *Mediaeval London*, © Timothy Baker 1970. Reprinted by permission of Cassell.

Hilaire Belloc: 'Rebecca, who slammed doors for fun and perished miserably' from *Cautionary Tales for Children*, © Hilaire Belloc 1908. Reprinted by permission of Peters, Fraser & Dunlop.

John Betjeman: 'Monody on the Death of Aldersgate Street Station' (*New Bats in Old Belfries* 1945) from *Collected Poems*, © John Betjeman 1958. Reprinted by permission of John Murray.

Michael Bond: *A Bear Called Paddington*, © Michael Bond 1958. Reprinted by permission of Lemon, Unna & Durbridge, published by HarperCollins.

Richard Church: 'Strap-hanging' from *Mood without Measure*, © Richard Church 1928. Reprinted by permission of Faber & Faber.

E.M. Forster: *Howard's End*, © E.M. Forster 1910. Reprinted by permission of King's College, Cambridge and The Society of Authors as literary representatives of the E.M. Forster Estate.

Robert Gray: *A History of London*, © Robert Gray 1978. Reprinted by permission of Hutchinson Books.

H. Howson: *London's Underground*, © H. Howson 1951 (first edition). Reprinted by permission of Ian Allan.

Aldous Huxley: *Crome Yellow*, © Aldous Huxley 1921. Reprinted by permission of Chatto & Windus.

Rose Macaulay: *Told by an Idiot*, © Rose Macaulay 1923. Reprinted by permission of Fraser & Dunlop.

A.A. Milne: 'Busy' from *Now We Are Six*, © A.A. Milne 1927. Reprinted by permission of Methuen Childrens Books.

ACKNOWLEDGEMENTS

John Mortimer: 'Rumpole and the Age of Retirement' from *The Trials of Rumpole*, © John Murray 1979. Reprinted by permission of Peters, Fraser & Dunlop.

H.V. Morton: *The Nights of London*, © H.V. Morton 1926. Reprinted by permission of Methuen London.

Iris Murdoch: *A Word Child*, © Iris Murdoch 1975. Reprinted by permission of Chatto & Windus.

Philippa Pearce: *A Dog So Small*, © Philippa Pearce 1962. Reprinted by permission of Constable.

J.B. Priestley: *Angel Pavement*, © J.B. Priestley 1930. Reprinted by permission of William Heinemann.

V.S. Pritchett: *A Cab at the Door*, © V.S. Pritchett 1968. *London Perceived*, © V.S. Pritchett 1962. Reprinted by permission of Chatto & Windus.

William Sansom: in *Living in London* edited by Alan Rose, © William Sansom 1974. Reprinted by permission of London Magazine.

Ben Weinreb and Christopher Hibbert: *The London Encyclopaedia*, © Ben Weinreb and Christopher Hibbert 1983. Reprinted by permission of Macmillan London.

H.G. Wells: 'The Diamond Maker' from *The Stolen Bacillus and Other Incidents*, © H.G. Wells 1895. Reprinted by permission of A.P. Watt on behalf of The Literary Executors of the Estate of H.G. Wells.

The publishers have made every effort to contact copyright holders where they can be found. The publishers will be happy to include any missing copyright acknowledgements in future editions.